Legends of Ten Chinese Traditional Festivals

中国十个节日传说

Illustrator *Zhan Tong*

编绘　詹同

Dolphin Books　　海豚

D0817394

Editor *Li Shufen He Wei*
Designer *Fang Yongming*

责任编辑　李树芬　何蔚
责任设计　房永明

中国十个节日传说
詹　同　编绘

出版　海豚出版社
　　　北京百万庄大街 24 号
邮编　100037
电话　010 - 68326332
传真　010 - 68993503
印刷　北京彩虹伟业印刷有限公司
发行　新华书店经销
版次　2010 年11月第 7 次印刷

ISBN 978-7-80138-003-6
定价　13.90 元

Spring Festival 春 节

The Spring Festival is the lunar Chinese New Year. Every family sets off firecrackers and puts up couplets on their gates to usher in a happy life in the coming year.

春节是中国农历的新年，家家贴对联、放鞭炮，庆贺在新的一年里生活幸福。

Long, long ago, there was a ferocious demon called *nian*. It did evil things everywhere.

传说在很古很古的时候，"年"是一只凶恶的怪兽，到处作恶。

The Heavenly God locked this demon into remote mountains and only allowed him to go out once a year.

天神将"年"这个怪兽锁进深山，只准它十二个月出山一次。

Shortly after twelve months had passed, *nian* came out of the mountains.

十二个月刚过完,"年"就出山来作恶。

Gathering together, people discussed how to deal with him. Some said that *nian* was afraid of the red color, flames, and noises.

大家商量对付它的办法。有人说"年"怕红颜色、怕火光、怕响声。

So people put up red couplets on their gates, set off firecrackers, and kept on beating gongs and drums.

于是人们在家门口贴红门联，放鞭炮，不停地敲锣打鼓。

The demon *nian* trembled with fear.

"年"吓得发抖。

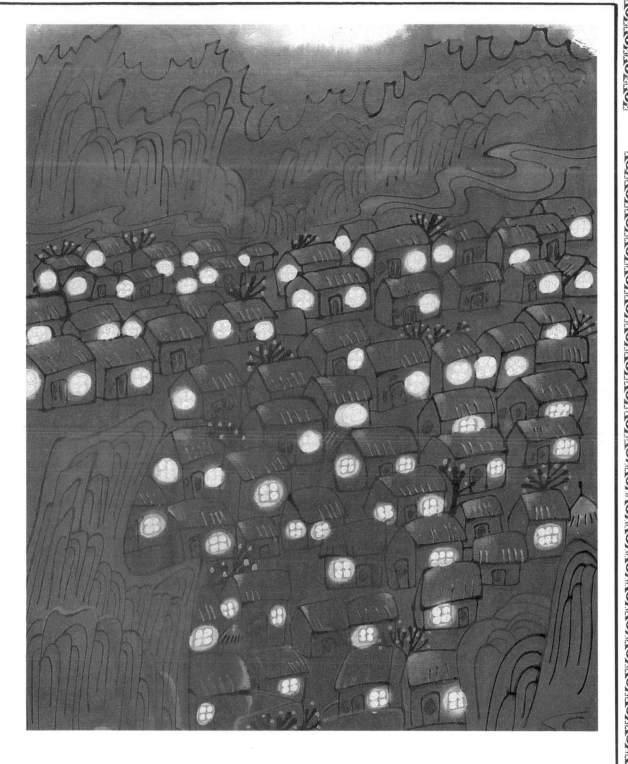

Night fell and every house was brightly lit.

到了晚上，家家灯火通明。

Nian was terrified. He fled into the mountains and didn't dare to come out.

"年"吓得胆颤心惊，逃回山里，再也不敢下山。

Nian was thus subdued, and the custom of celebrating the lunar New Year was passed down from then.

"年"被制服了。但庆贺农历新年的习惯却流传下来，一直到现在。

Lantern Festival 灯　节

The fifteenth day of the first lunar month is the day of the Lantern Festival. This festival dates back over 2,000 years.

农历正月十五是中国灯节。两千多年前就有这个风俗。

The Jade Emperor in Heaven lived comfortably, but he felt very lonely.

传说天宫里的玉皇大帝生活很舒适，但非常寂寞。

When he learned that people on earth lived happily, he got quite angry.

玉帝听说人间生活快乐、幸福,非常生气。

He decided to send the Magic Goose who could breathe out flames to burn up the world on the fifteenth day of the first lunar month.

因此他派会喷火的神鹅在正月十五日这一天晚上来到人间,要把人间烧光。

A kind-hearted maid of the Heavenly Palace went down to the world hurriedly and told everybody about the news.

天宫里一位好心的宫女赶快来到人间，把这个消息告诉了大家。

A clever man got an idea. He called up his fellow citizens to make red lanterns immediately.

一个聪明人想了个办法，让大家赶快扎制红灯。

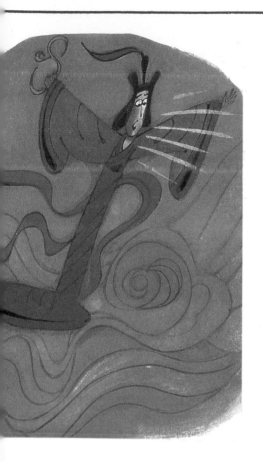

The maid also told people that once the Magic Goose was caged, it would no longer be able to breathe out flames.

宫女又告诉大家,只要把神鹅关在笼子里,它就不能喷火。

Shortly after it landed on the earth, and before it got the chance to start a fire, the Magic Goose was caught and caged.

神鹅刚刚着地,还没来得及喷火,就被人们捉进笼子里。

People then lit their lanterns and set off fireworks and firecrackers. When the Jade Emperor saw the flame, he thought it was the fire set by the Magic Goose, so he became very happy.

大家赶快点上灯，又燃放焰火、花炮。玉皇大帝看到人间四处是火光，以为神鹅放火了，心里十分高兴。

In fact, people were holding lanterns to celebrate their victory. Later, when this day came, every family made lanterns and held them. So the fifteenth day of the first lunar month became known as the Lantern Festival.

其实是人们举着灯在庆祝胜利。后来，每到这一天，家家挂灯、人人举灯，于是人们就把这一天叫作灯节。

Dragon Head Festival
龙头节

The Dragon Head Festival, celebrated in rural China, falls on the second day of the second lunar month. The Chinese proverb "on the second day of the second lunar month the dragon raises its head" has a story behind it.

农历二月二日是中国农村的"龙头节"。"二月二，龙抬头"。这个谚语说的是下面一个故事。

Long ago, in an ancient time, there was a drought along the Yellow River that lasted for three years. All the rivers had dried up and people suffered a lot.

古时候，黄河一带三年大旱，河水干涸了。人们痛苦极了。

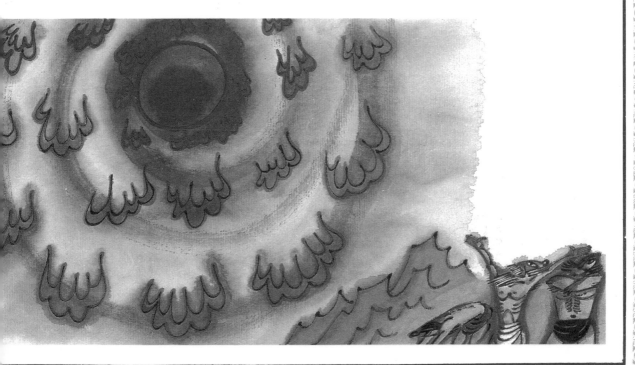

There was a mountain called Dragon Ax on the bank of the Yellow River. At the foot of the mountain lived a young couple. The man was called Qiang Wa and the woman Long Hua.

黄河边上有一座龙斧山，山下住着小俩口，男的叫强娃，女的叫龙花。

Both Qiang Wa and Long Hua were determined to look for sources of water to help their fellow villagers. An old man told them that they could find water at the bottom of the Golden Dragon Pond.

他们俩决心为人们找水源。有位老人告诉他们只有在金龙潭底才能挖出水来。

Qiang Wa and Long Hua were not afraid of difficulties or hardships. They kept on crawling until they reached the bottom of the Golden Dragon Pond.

强娃和龙花不怕艰难,爬呀爬呀,一直爬到金龙潭底。

They didn't stop digging for forty-nine days. One day they dug out a white, round stone from the earth. With one roll, the stone suddenly turned into a white dove and flew up.

他俩在潭底挖了 49 天，挖出了一个白石头蛋。一翻滚，突然变成一只白鸽子飞了起来。

The dove landed on the side of the pond and turned into an old man with a white beard. The old man said, "Good children, hurry to the top of the Dragon Ax Mountain and try to get the mountain-cutting ax. With this ax you can cut through the mountain and let in the water." Having said this, the old man turned into a cloud of white smoke and disappeared.

白鸽飞到潭边，又变成一个白胡子老人。老人说："好孩子，你们快去龙斧山寻找劈山斧，劈开山就有水了。"说完变成一股白烟消失了。

After many, many hardships, Qiang Wa and Long Hua reached the top of the Dragon Ax Mountain. There they saw a small temple.

强娃和龙花费尽千辛万苦爬上龙斧山，山顶上有一座小庙。

They went into the temple and found a big ax. Shouldering it, they hurried back to the Golden Dragon Pond.

他俩走进庙门，找到一把大斧头，扛着大斧赶忙回到金龙潭。

Qiang Wa swung one blow
the mountain, and with a loud noise
a stream of spring water spurted ou
A golden dragon rushed to the sk
and at once raindrops fell to th
ground.

强娃举斧一砍，一声巨响，潭
喷出一股清水，一条金龙冲上天空
立刻下起了大雨。

So people named the second day of
the second lunar month the Dragon
Head Festival in honor of the golden
dragon.

为了纪念金龙下雨，人们约定二月
二日这一天为龙头节。

Clear and Bright Festival
清明节

The Clear and Bright Festival is celebrated every year on a day in early April. On that day, people usually go on outings, pay respects to the ancestors at their tombs, wear flowers, and plant willow twigs into the ground.

　　每年四月初的某一日是中国的清明节。这一天，人们郊游、扫墓、戴花和插柳。

During the Spring and Autumn Period some 2,500 years ago, Chong Er, son of the Duke of the State of Jin, was forced to live in exile for some nineteen years. But later he became the Duke.

早在公元前的春秋时代，晋国公子重耳流亡 19 年后，回国做了国君。

He granted titles and fiefdoms to those who had followed him throughout his exile.

他封赏和他一齐流亡的随从人员。

One follower called Jie Zhitui was forgotten by Chong Er. Jie Zhitui then carried his mother on his back and hid in the Mianshan Mountain.

有个叫介之推的人被重耳遗忘了,便背着母亲躲进绵山。

Someone reminded Chong Er of Jie Zhitui.

有人提醒重耳。

Chong Er sent people to look for Jie, but they all failed because the Mianshan Mountain was too large.

重耳派人去找介之推,但绵山太大,无法找到。

Then one man suggested, "Set the mountain on fire，and Jie Zhitui will certainly come out."Chong Er ordered a fire to be set to the mountain.

又有人说:"放一把火,介之推就会逃出来。"重耳下令火烧绵山。

The fire spread all over the mountain, but Jie Zhitui still would not come out. Finally he and his mother were burned to death.

大火烧遍了绵山,介之推和老母仍不肯出山,最后烧死了。

Chong Er felt very sad. He is-
sued an order that every family put
out their kitchen fire and eat cold
food that very day.

重耳非常难过,命令从此这天
不许点火,家家都吃"寒食"。(即吃
冷东西)

The custom of putting out the kitchen
fire on the Clear and Bright Festival has
vanished, but the habits of planting willow
twigs and paying respects to ancestors at
their tombs have continued to the present
day.

清明节禁火的习惯已经没有了。但种
柳、扫墓纪念先辈等习惯一直流传至今。

Dragon Boat Festival

端午节

The Dragon Boat Festival falls on the fifth day of the fifth lunar month. On that day, every family in rural China eats *zongzi* (glutinous rice wrapped in reed leaves). It is also the custom to hang wormwood and carry "fragrant pouches" made of bits of cloth wound with colored silk threads.

农历五月五日是端午节。这一天，中国农村家家吃粽子、带香包、插艾蒿。

Why do people eat *zongzi*? It is said to be done in memory of Qu Yuan.

为什么要吃粽子呢？人们说是为了纪念屈原。

Qu Yuan was a high-ranking official of the State of Chu during the Warring States Period (475-221 B. C.). He had made great contributions to the state.

屈原是春秋时楚国的大官,曾经建立过很多功绩。

The corrupt officials of the court slandered Qu Yuan until finally he was removed from office by the Duke.

由于奸臣的陷害,被国王革职。

Later he was banished and led a wandering life.

以后又被放逐,过着流浪生活。

He still loved his country and people and was overwhelmed with sadness.

他忧国忧民,悲愤之极。

Qu Yuan drowned himself in the Miluo River on the fifth day of the fifth lunar month upon the news of his country being conquered.

五月五日这一天，屈原跳进汨罗江自杀，用生命激起人民热情。

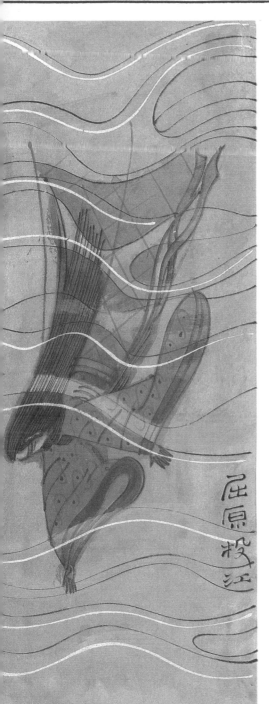

The People of the State of Chu threw rice into the river as a sacrifice to him.

楚国百姓把米投入江中，祭祀屈原。

Later they were afraid that the fish and shrimps would eat the rice. So they wrapped the food in reed leaves and wound silk threads around the packets before dropping them into the river.

后来又怕米被鱼虾吃去,便用苇叶将米包起,用丝线扎紧,制成粽子投入江里。

People also used bits of cloth to make "fragrant pouches" wound round with colored silk threads and carried them. They hung calamus and wormwood, which are two medicinal herbs, on their gates to symbolize a knife and sword to conquer evil.

人们又用五色丝线制成香包挂在身上，又用菖蒲，艾蒿插在门首，象征刀剑，镇服邪恶。

Double Seventh Night 七夕节

The Double Seventh Night falls on the seventh night of the seventh lunar month. On that night girls hold needle-threading competitions to see who has nimble fingers. The competitions are held in honor of the weaving maid of the Heavenly Palace.

农历七月七日是"七夕节"。这一天夜间女孩们比赛彩线穿针,看谁手巧,纪念天宫里的织女。

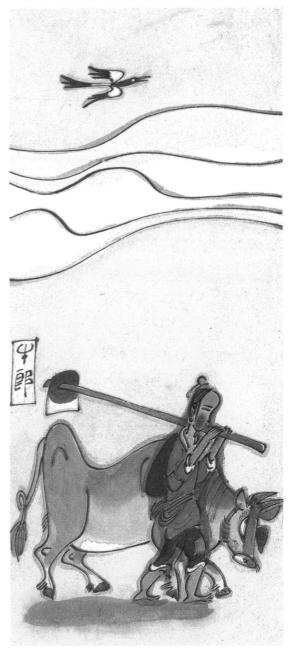

The weaving maid in the Heavenly Palace wove celestial brocade for the Queen Mother of the Western Heaven every day.

天宫里有一位织女,天天为王母娘娘织锦。

On earth there lived a cowherd who led a miserable life. He had only one companion—an old ox.

人间有一个牛郎,生活很苦,只有一头老黄牛和他相依为命。

The weaving maid fell in love with the cowherd because he was so hard-working. Stealthily, she went down to the world and married him. Later she gave birth to a boy and a girl, and the family lived happily together.

织女爱牛郎勤劳，偷偷来到人间和他结了婚，生了一男一女，过着幸福、美满的日子。

The Queen Mother of the Western Heaven got very angry and ordered troops from the heaven to bring back the weaving maid.

王母娘娘发了火，命令天神捉回织女。

The heavenly force captured the weaving maid. Holding the children, the cowherd chased after them on the back of the old ox.

天神抓走织女。牛郎骑着老黄牛，抱着两个孩子在后面追赶。

The Queen Mother of the Western Heaven plucked a gold pin from her hair and drew a line with it in the air. Immediately a celestial river appeared in the sky. The cowherd and the weaving maid were separated by the river.

王母娘娘拔下头上的金簪,当空一划,立刻出现一条天河,把牛郎、织女隔在两岸。

On the seventh night of the seventh lunar month every year, magpies fly to the river and form a bridge over it , and the cowherd and weaving maid meet in the middle of the bridge.

每年七月七日喜鹊在河上搭成了桥，让牛郎和织女相会。

On that night, girls beg the weaving maid to pass them skill at weaving. They also rejoice at the couple's reunion.

这天晚上，女孩儿们乞望从织女那儿学来织锦手艺，也为牛郎、织女相会而欢乐。

Mid-Autumn Festival
中 秋 节

The Mid-Autumn Festival falls on the fifteenth day of the eighth lunar month. On that day every family eats mooncakes. Children usually buy different kinds of clay toys.

农历八月十五是中秋节。这一天家家吃月饼，孩子们购买泥玩具"兔儿爷"。

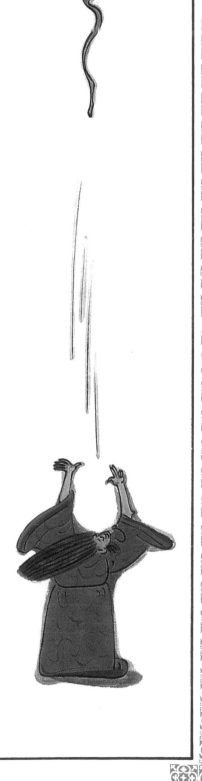

The story below is one of the many legends about the Mid-Autumn Festival.

中秋节的传说很多,这儿只讲其中的一个。

A Taoist priest said to the Tang Emperor Xuan Zong, "I can take you to the moon palace." Having said this, he threw his walking stick into the sky.

有个道人对唐明皇说:"我有办法让你去月宫游玩。"说着将拐杖扔上天空。

The stick turned into a long bridge. The Tang Emperor followed the priest onto the passage and entered the moon palace.

拐杖在天空化成一座长桥。唐明皇随着道人走上桥去,走进月宫。

In the moon palace, the Tang Emperor saw a Jade Rabbit pounding medicinal herbs in a mortar and a group of fairy maidens dancing and playing music. Fascinated by the music the Tang Emperor tried to remember the tunes by heart.

在月宫里，唐明皇看见玉兔在捣药，仙女们跳舞、奏乐，便记下了这些优美曲调。

After returning to the world, the emperor composed a song-and-dance piece called "Rainbow Petticoats and Feather Dresses" after the tunes he brought back in his memory from the moon palace.

回到人间，唐明皇按照月宫里的曲调编排了一个歌舞曲"霓裳羽衣曲"。

Double Ninth Day 重阳节

The ninth day of the ninth lunar month is known as the Double Ninth Day. On that day people usually go traveling or climbing mountains.

农历九月九日叫"重阳节"。这一天,人们都习惯旅行、登山。

During the Eastern Han Dynasty (25-220 A. D.) there was a Taoist priest called Fei Changfang. he knew magic arts and could drive out evil spirits.

汉代有一个人叫费长房,很有法术,能驱神捉鬼。

One day Fei Changfang warned his disciple Huan Jing that the spirit of disaster would visit the world on the ninth day of the ninth lunar month. Fei told Huan Jing to go to the countryside and conquer it.

一天,费长房对弟子桓景说,九月九日瘟疫魔鬼要在人间作乱,要他去乡间除害。

Fei gave Huan Jing a parcel containing the leaves of a medicinal cornel plant and a jug of chrysanthemum wine. He asked his disciple to take them to the people.

他又拿出茱萸（中草药）一包、菊花壶一把，叫桓景带着给百姓。

Riding on a white crane, Huan Jing descended to the world.

桓景骑上白鹤飞向乡间。

He led people up a mountain and gave everyone a cornel leaf and a drink of chrysanthemum wine. These would prevent the disaster from getting near.

他带着人们登上高山，给每人一片茱萸叶子，一口菊花酒。这样瘟疫魔鬼就不敢近身。

Disaster came to the village. It found no one there. Catching sight of the people on the mountain it rushed to the mountain.

瘟魔来了,冲入村庄,不见人影。它见人们都在高山上,立即冲上山去。

Unexpectedly it caught a whiff of chrysanthemum wine and cornel plant. Hesitating to go ahead, it was stabbed by Huan Jing and fell to the ground.

瘟魔忽然闻到酒气刺鼻。茱萸香味又逼来,不敢上前。桓景一剑将它刺倒在地。

Since then people have gone traveling or climbing, bringing along chrysanthemum wine and twigs of the cornel plant, on the ninth day of the ninth lunar month.

从此,人们每到九月九日,都带着菊花酒,臂插茱萸,外出旅行、登高。

Laba Festival 腊八节

On the eighth day of the twelfth lunar month, the Laba Festival is celebrated. On that day every family eats *laba* congee(The twelfth lunar month is called the *la* month, which means a world of ice and snow).

农历十二月八日,是中国的腊八节。这天家家吃腊八粥。(十二月称腊月,是天冷、冰雪的世界之意)

Long, long ago, there was a
family of four: an old couple and a
young couple who lived happily together.

从前，有这么一家人，老两口
和小两口过日子，很快活。

The old couple did all the housework. They didn't
let the young couple do anything, for fear of them getting
tired.

老两口什么活也不让小两口干，怕他们俩累着。

The young couple led and easy life with everything provided for them. They did not know how to do anything.

小两口整天饭来张口、衣来伸手，什么事也不会干。

Later the old couple died. After eating up all the food that had been stored in the house, the young couple sold their house and was left with only half a broken straw shed.

后来，老两口去世了。小两口把家里的粮食吃光了，把房子也卖了，只剩下了半间烂草棚。

Winter came. The couple suffered from cold and hunger in their poor shelter.

冬天来了,小两口连冻带饿,躲在草棚里发抖。

On the eighth day of the twelfth lunar month, when they could bear the hunger no more, they scrounged up a little grain from the corners of the shed and cooked a pot of congee.

到了腊月初八这一天,他们实在饿得受不住了,就从草棚角落扫出一点杂粮来,熬了一点稀粥。

A gust of wind blew down their shed and they were crushed to death.

一阵大风吹来，把草棚吹倒了，小两口就被压死了。

People learned about this later. In order to teach their children about the sad fate of that lazy couple, they would cook congee with all kinds of grains and , while eating it, tell the story.

人们知道这件事。为了让孩子们记住这个教训，在腊月初八这一天，用各种杂粮合在一起熬一锅粥，边吃边说这个故事。

Kitchen God Day 祭灶

On the twenty-third day of the twelfth lunar month, children eat melon-shaped candies and adults offer melon-shaped candies as a sacrifice to the Kitchen God.

农历十二月二十三这天，孩子们吃糖瓜。大人用糖瓜供奉灶王。

Long, long ago, there was a lord. He was very fond of eating. He had soon tasted all the delicious foods in his palace.

传说从前有一个王爷很贪吃，天下的好东西他都捞着吃了。

Later he went out of his palace to look for good things to eat.

后来，他走出王宫，到各家各户找好东西吃。

He came to a woman's house and begged for food.
他来到一位大嫂家里，开口就讨东西吃。

He soon ate up the sugar cakes the woman had baked.
大嫂烙的糖饼全让王爷吃光了。

Then he asked the woman to go to his palace with him and bake sugar cakes for him every day.

王爷还要大嫂进宫整天给他烙糖饼吃。

The woman wouldn't hear of it. The lord then threatened to drag her to the palace.

大嫂不肯,王爷就动手,要把她拉进皇宫。

The woman lost her temper and slapped him on the face with all her might. The slap sent the lord flying to the wall behind the kitchen sink.

大嫂生了气，一巴掌把王爷扇到锅台后面的墙上去了。

The woman said to the lord, "Stop being such a glutton! Stay there and watch other people eat!" From then on the lord couldn't get down. Later he became the Kitchen God.

大嫂说："叫你嘴馋。让你每天站在这儿只能看着别人吃好东西。"从此，王爷就下不来了。后来成了灶王。

People worried that the Kitchen God might report bad things about them to the Heavenly God. So every year, before the Spring Festival, they would post a new picture of the Kitchen God and offer him melon-shaped candies. Now people no longer post the pictures, but children still get melon-shaped candies to eat.

人们怕灶王说坏话，每年春节前给他贴新的画像，用糖瓜供奉他。如今人们不再贴灶王了，但孩子们照常吃糖瓜。